What Do You Mean?

What Do You Mean?

A Story about Noah Webster

by Jeri Ferris

illustrations by Steve Michaels

A Carolrhoda Creative Minds Book

Carolrhoda Books, Inc./Minneapolis

For my son Tom
A wordsmith too

The author wishes to thank the director and staff of the Noah
Webster Foundation, West Hartford, Connecticut, and Howard
B. Field, great-great-grandson of Noah Webster, for their invalu-
able assistance.

Library of Congress Cataloging-in-Publication Data

Ferris, Jeri.
    What do you mean? : a story about Noah Webster / by Jeri Ferris ;
illustrations by Steve Michaels.
        p.   cm. — (A Carolrhoda creative minds book)
    Summary: Traces the life of the farm boy who became a teacher and
went on to write the first American dictionary.
    ISBN 0-87614-330-3 (lib. bdg.)
    1. Webster, Noah, 1758-1843 — Juvenile literature.
2. Lexicographers — United States — Biography — Juvenile literature.
3. Educators — United States — Biography — Juvenile literature.
[1. Webster, Noah, 1758-1843. 2. Lexicographers. 3. Teachers.]
I. Michaels, Steve, ill. II. Title. III. Series.
PE64.W5F48   1988
423'.092'4 — dc19
[B]
[92]   88-5420
                                               CIP
                                               AC

Manufactured in the United States of America

1 2 3 4 5 6 7 8 9 10 98 97 96 95 94 93 92 91 90 89 88

Table of Contents

INTRODUCTION

Back in the days when most folks were farmers, Noah Webster was born (on a farm) in West Hartford, Connecticut. His family was descended from a long line of Pilgrims and Puritans, of whom they were very proud—except for the one relative who was executed in 1654 for being a witch. But that relative died long before Noah was born, 104 years before to be exact.

The small, white house in which Noah grew up had only four rooms, but the 80-acre farm was big enough for the Websters to raise everything they needed. They grew wheat, corn, oats, tobacco, and flax. They had pigs, sheep, cows, oxen, and horses. And there was an orchard with lots of apple trees.

Noah had chores to do every day. Six days a week, he fed the pigs and sheep and cows and oxen and horses, chopped the wood for the fireplace, and helped plant or weed or harvest the crops. On Sundays, the Webster family went to church and visited with their neighbors (and Noah fed the pigs and sheep and cows and oxen and horses).

After church, the farmers would often talk about the king of England and how he was treating his American colonies. They said he wasn't treating them very well. King George needed money, and he wanted to get it by taxing the colonists. The colonists began to wonder if King George had a right to do this.

Noah decided he didn't like King George.

But meanwhile, there was farming to be done. So Noah went on learning how to be a farmer, summer and winter, before and after school. By the time he was 12, in 1770, Noah knew how to grow or make almost everything his family needed. He even knew how to weave cloth for a shirt or a blanket. His father was pleased. He said Noah would be a fine farmer, following in the footsteps of a long line of Webster farmers.

But Noah did not *want* to be in that long line. He didn't want to be a farmer at all.

Chapter One

Noah Webster looked at his almanac. March 1770, snow, it said. He sat down to write at the copy desk at the front of the schoolroom.

"First class! Stand!" the teacher roared. The youngest children jumped up.

"Spell *little.*" The teacher hit the top of his desk with a switch.

"L-I-T, lit, T-L-E, tle, little!" the children shouted.

After the spelling lesson, it was time for Noah's younger brother, Charles, to recite his lesson.

Noah held his breath as Charles walked slowly up to the teacher. Poor Charles, thought Noah, he had tried so hard to learn the whole psalm, but he just couldn't remember it. The teacher waited, with his switch in one hand and a book in the other, while Charles stared at the dirt floor. Finally, the teacher gave Charles a hard swat and ordered him to take his book to the corner, away from the fire.

Noah's face got hot, and he bit his lip to keep the words in. He picked up the quill pen, dipped it into the ink bottle, and carefully started to write *mor-ti-fi-ca-ti-on,* one of the hardest words in the spelling book. But he saw Charles shivering in the corner and pushed too hard on his pen. The ink spot on his neat paper made him even madder.

Finally, school was over. Noah waited outside for Charles. The snow crunched under his boots as he marched around to keep warm. In the west, the sun was sinking toward the soft blue hills. In the east, Noah could see the little town of Hartford on the Connecticut River. Its houses were all bunched together as if they were trying to keep warm.

At last Charles came out, and the two boys

raced for home. As they passed the pig shed, they saw their older brother, Abraham, feeding the pigs. Noah knew they were late, but the words he had stored up all day couldn't wait.

"Mother," Noah called as he dashed in the kitchen door. He shook the snow off his coat and hurried to the fire. "Mother, Charles got a licking from the teacher after school."

Noah's mother looked up from the apple dumplings she was making. "Don't stop to talk now, Noah. Abraham has already started your chores."

"Is the newspaper here?" Noah put his coat back on. "I want to find out what happened in Boston after King George's soldiers shot those men. I think . . ."

But Noah's mother didn't let him finish. She wiped the flour from her hands and pointed to the door.

Abraham didn't want to hear Noah's ideas either. So Noah thought to himself as he fed the animals and chopped wood. Why did King George have to send soldiers to America anyway? And why were they shooting at colonists? Noah finished his chores and hurried back to the house. Maybe his father felt like listening to his ideas.

That year, Noah completed all the classes there

were at the school in West Hartford, but he wanted to study some more. His father agreed to let him study Latin and Greek with the Reverend Nathan Perkins if he promised to keep up his share of the farm work. Noah promised.

By the spring of 1773, there were even more British soldiers in America, but, happily for Noah and his family, the soldiers left Hartford alone. Unhappily, Noah was having a hard time keeping his promise.

One fine afternoon, Noah had his nose deep in a book of Latin grammar when he heard his father calling. He jumped up. The horses were right there where he'd left them. So were the stone-filled wagon and the half-finished stone wall. The closer Mr. Webster got to Noah and the unfinished wall and the book, the angrier he looked. He scrutinized the wall, sighed, took the book out of Noah's hand, and closed it firmly.

Noah was ashamed. For once he didn't have anything to say. He looked over the stone wall at the flowering apple trees in the orchard, took a deep breath of the sweet-smelling spring air, and went to the wagon for more stones. I *still* don't want to farm, Noah thought. But a promise is a promise.

Noah finished the wall just before dark. Then he rode over to see Reverend Perkins. He explained that his father was not happy with him because he studied more than he farmed and didn't always finish his share of the farm work as he had promised. Abraham was not happy because their father was spending money on Noah's studies instead of horses or corn. And he, Noah, was not happy because what he really wanted to do was read and learn.

Reverend Perkins agreed that Noah was not cut out for farming. In fact, Noah's tutor had a revolutionary idea. He thought Noah should go to the best school in Connecticut—Yale.

"Impossible," Noah said. "How could I ever get the money? My father has spent all his money to let me study with you, and you know how my brother feels. But to go to Yale..."

Chapter Two

In September 1774, Noah walked down the dusty road from Hartford toward Yale College in New Haven. His father rode beside him on his horse. All three of them looked tired after their journey. Their long shadows, made by the late afternoon sun, seemed to lie wearily on the ground.

For two days and 50 miles, Noah had been trying to find just the right words to thank his father. After all, Mr. Webster had mortgaged his whole farm to raise enough money to send his son to Yale. Noah's throat tightened every time he thought of the thanks (and the money) he owed his father. Of course, before they parted, Noah managed to find the words he was looking for, and he promised to pay back all the money, too.

A week later, the morning bell rang at 5:30 in Connecticut Hall. Noah and his new friend Joel Barlow hurried to get to prayers on time (the professors took it very seriously if the boys were late). After prayers, they dashed to breakfast in the big dining hall.

Breakfast was just biscuits and coffee, and if there was anything Noah and Joel didn't like, it was coffee. In fact, most American colonists disliked coffee. What they all really wanted was a good dish of English tea, which is what they used to drink before the trouble with England. But King George demanded that the colonists pay a tax on his tea (and on paint and paper and glass), and this they refused to do. So they drank coffee instead and hated it and King George.

Noah told Joel that his father said he was born "in a time of war and trouble." Why, wondered Noah, should the colonists be ruled by a king who lived so far away? Maybe, Noah said, they shouldn't be.

That spring, Noah heard about the battle at Lexington and Concord between British redcoats and American minutemen. By June, the students at Yale had spent more time marching around the green and talking about the war than they had spent studying. When General George Washington rode through New Haven on his fine white horse to take command of the new American army, the students marched proudly beside him.

18

Noah, in his best black suit, led the way playing "Yankee Doodle" on his flute.

By 1776, Noah's second year at Yale, the colonists realized that King George was not going to call his soldiers back to England. They decided, at last, that they didn't want a king at all. They wanted to be independent. In Philadelphia, Thomas Jefferson wrote the Declaration of Independence to tell the whole world that the 13 American colonies had broken their bonds with England, and why. The men of the Continental Congress approved the Declaration on July 4, 1776. King George, of course, did *not* approve it. He didn't want to give up his American colonies, and he sent more soldiers to show the colonists that he really meant it.

In August 1776, because of the disruptions of the war, Noah and his classmates were still at Yale. And, as usual, Noah was as busy telling people his opinions as he was studying. Then a typhoid epidemic struck New Haven. Yale was closed until November, and Noah walked the 50 miles back home.

When Noah appeared unexpectedly at the kitchen door, Mrs. Webster almost dropped the glass lantern she was lighting. Noah gave her a hug and explained that all the students had been sent home because of an epidemic in New Haven.

"Have you any news of Abraham?" Noah went on, pulling off his heavy boots. "I heard he was captured by the British."

His mother smiled. "He can tell you himself," she said as Abraham came into the kitchen. Mr. Webster and Charles were right behind him, stamping the dirt from the fields off their boots.

Noah had a lot of questions for Abraham. Abraham did his best to squeeze in the answers. Yes, it was true he had been captured. No, he had not escaped, he had come down with smallpox. The British didn't want a prisoner with smallpox, so they had let him go. Now he was just fine and was riding back to join his troops the next day. "In fact," said Abraham, "you can come with me and bring the horse back home."

Before Noah could spell *re-vo-lu-ti-on,* he was on his way north to Lake Champlain with Abraham and the horse and the other men going to fight the British.

After a few days of choking on the dust kicked up by the horses and soldiers, Noah gave up trying to talk. He kept his mouth shut, with a rag over it so he could breathe.

After a few nights of trying to sleep outside, Noah gave up swatting mosquitoes. He moved inside the tent with Abraham and the smoky stove that kept the mosquitoes away.

A few days later, Noah rode back home again.

When he returned to school for his third year, Noah told his friends about marching with real soldiers. Even though he wasn't in any battles, he said, it was awful. No, it was worse than awful, it was horrendous.

Meanwhile, the British soldiers were eating a lot of the corn and wheat and meat that belonged to the colonists. There was very little food for General Washington's army.

In March 1777, the students were sent home again for a month. There was not much food left anywhere in Connecticut and no food at all at Yale. When the Websters had used the last of their sugar, Noah helped his father crush cornstalks and boil the juice. This made a kind of sugar, but it tasted strange to Noah's sweet tooth.

The fighting spread to Connecticut in April, and Noah's whole class was moved away from New Haven to the little town of Glastonbury, near Hartford, for safety. All that summer, the Americans tried to stop General Burgoyne and his British troops from taking New England; and all that summer, Noah tried to study. In September, when classes ended, Noah decided to join his father and two brothers and the rest of the Connecticut militia when they went to fight Burgoyne in New York. Noah told his father, who was the captain of the West Hartford militia, that he wanted to push the British out of America for good.

Charles heard this and laughed. "Maybe if you threaten to talk to them they'll leave, Noah." Noah's face reddened, but he laughed, too. He knew everyone thought he talked a lot.

A few weeks later, Noah marched up the Hudson River with his father's troops, but Burgoyne was defeated at the Battle of Saratoga before they got there. Noah marched back home. He never did get to fight the British.

November 1777 was the beginning of Noah's last year at Yale as well as the beginning of a bitterly cold winter in New England. The British soldiers waited out that long, cold winter in Philadelphia and kept warm. Meanwhile, General Washington and his hungry, barefoot, freezing troops camped in ragged tents and log huts in nearby Valley Forge.

When spring came, the fighting began again. Noah's class had to move from place to place that summer to stay out of the way of the fighting. But in September, at last, Noah, Joel, and the rest of their classmates graduated from Yale.

After graduation, Noah hurried home to Hartford. He had to decide what to do next. Should he join the army? Study to be a lawyer? Go back to farming? Noah owed his father a lot of money, and his father needed it. He knew he had to find a job fast.

Chapter Three

That winter, 19-year-old Noah was back in a one-room schoolhouse. The school in Glastonbury had a dirt floor, a fireplace, and a new teacher— Mr. Noah Webster.

Noah had no blackboard, no chalk, no pencils, no maps, and hardly any books. But he had plenty of students. He had little ones who were just learning the ABCs and big ones who already knew how to read and write and figure.

The students wrote with quill pens made of goose feathers and with ink made of mashed, boiled walnut shells. The youngest class read "ab-eb-ib-ob-ub," "ba-be-bi-bo-bu," and "I am to go in" out loud. At the same time, the older boys and girls read longer words out loud. The oldest boys and girls made scratching noises with their pens as they carefully wrote out the longest words of all. And the roar of the wood burning in the fireplace filled any tiny pocket of quiet that was left over.

Before long, Noah decided he didn't want to teach. He wanted to be a lawyer. But how could he study law *and* still make enough money to pay back his father and pay his own bills? When the school year was over, Noah moved to Hartford. He tried teaching all day and studying all night. By fall, he had learned a little law, but he had also slept only a little. He decided to go back to teaching all day and sleeping all night.

That winter, Noah moved back to his family's farm and got a job teaching at a little school four miles from home. Unfortunately for Noah, it was the coldest winter in years. The snow was so deep it covered the tops of the fences. Every morning, Noah put on the warmest coat and thickest scarf he had and set off through the snow on foot. All day long, he tried to teach his students to read, with hardly any books, and to write, with no pencils or chalk, and to find far-away places like Africa, with no maps. It was very discouraging. Worst of all, Noah wasn't earning enough money to pay back his father.

Noah really did like to teach after all, but he thought that there should be a better way for students to learn. It would certainly help to have books and maps and desks and smaller classes. The few books they did have came from England, while Americans were fighting to be free from England. There were no American school-books at all.

The next summer, 1780, Noah went back to studying law and got a job in a law office. But whenever he wasn't studying and whenever he wasn't working in the law office, he was thinking about the terrible schools in America.

Noah passed his last exam in the spring of 1781 and became a lawyer. Now he could sign his name "Noah Webster, Jr., Esquire, Attorney-at-Law." He liked the sound of this long name so much that he used it on almost everything he wrote.

He opened his law office in Hartford and waited for clients. He waited and waited. At last, Noah decided that Americans were too busy with the war to need a lawyer. He'd be a lawyer later. For now, he would go back to teaching, but this time, he would open his *own* school.

Noah chose the town of Sharon, in northwestern Connecticut, for his school. In June, he put an ad in the *Connecticut Courant:*

[To] promote Education, so essential to the interest of a free people, [I propose] immediately to open a school at Sharon, in which young Gentlemen and Ladies may be instructed in Reading, Writing, Mathematicks . . . by the public's very humble servant, Noah Webster, Jun.

Some of the richest families in town sent their children to Noah Webster's school. Noah's teaching was based on his own good ideas, but he still had to use British schoolbooks. Noah began to write down some of his ideas about how children should be taught. He spent nearly all of his money on paper and ink and on his school. He had little left over to send to his father and almost none at all for himself. But his school seemed to be doing well.

Then one day, Noah overheard two of his students talking. They were talking about him. They laughed about his wild red hair and the way his long arms and legs stuck out of his clothes.

Noah's face burned. He tugged at his cuffs, but it was no use. His clothes were too old and too small, and he had no money to replace them.

He picked up his books, stuck out his chin, and marched into the classroom. The girls in their fancy linen dresses all seemed to be laughing silently. The boys in their fine woolen coats all seemed to be smiling behind their books. Noah taught the geography lesson and dismissed the class.

Two days later, he closed his school.

Chapter Four

In October 1781, the British soldiers finally gave up. The revolutionary war was over, and America was free from England at last. That winter, Noah didn't teach school. He didn't reopen his law office. Instead, he looked for another job and studied French, German, Spanish, Italian, history, and politics.

Noah still hadn't found a job by spring, so he decided to reopen his school in Sharon. But people remembered that he had closed his first school, and on opening day, no one came.

Noah was so embarrassed that he packed his things, crossed the Hudson River, and found a room in a boardinghouse in Goshen, New York. That night, Noah shook out his pockets. He had only 75¢ left. He thought about all the money he owed his father. He thought about Noah Webster, Jr., Esquire, Attorney-at-Law with no clients. Then he thought about American schools without American books, and before he could spell *i-de-a,* he had one.

He, Noah Webster, would teach Americans how to read and write and speak and spell the American way. *He* would write schoolbooks for America.

Noah opened his ink bottle. He wrote that America had declared its independence from England, but it needed to be independent in ideas, too. Noah jumped up. His thoughts were coming too fast for his pen.

"I will write the second Declaration of Independence," Noah cried, "an American spelling book!"

Noah couldn't live on 75¢ for long, so he took a teaching job in Goshen. He taught all day and worked on his spelling book at night. He wrote his friend Joel about his plans.

Noah said that now that they had a new, free country, they also needed a new way of teaching Americans. He said that they needed to have *American* schoolbooks. They needed good books and good teachers in every little schoolhouse.

In his reply, Joel agreed there was a need for American books, but he thought it would be hard to convince people to use Noah's speller instead of Dilworth's. Noah frowned when he read this.

Dilworth's speller was the one he and Abraham and Charles had used. American schools still used it, even though it talked about London and England and kings and queens.

Joel's letter went on to say that printers didn't have to pay for the right to print Dilworth's speller, so they kept printing it.

Noah sat back. Joel was right. His speller would have to be so good that Americans would buy it instead of the book they were used to. And there was another problem. What would keep printers from copying his book over and over without paying him, as they did with Dilworth's?

In October 1782, before the spelling book was finished, Noah wrote to the General Assembly of Connecticut. He asked the lawmakers to pass a law giving the author of a book, and only the author, the right to sell that book. Then Noah rode to Pennsylvania, New Jersey, and New York to ask those states to pass the same law. By the spring of 1783, several states had passed the new "copyright" law.

Now Noah had to find someone to print his spelling book. The publishers of the *Courant* in Hartford agreed to do it if Noah would pay for the printing and allow them to print future editions of the book. Joel lent him the money, and Noah moved back to Hartford to watch over the printing of his speller. At night, he worked on his next two projects, a grammar book and a reading book.

Noah's spelling book came out in October 1783. It cost a lot—14¢—but it took off like a hot-air balloon.

In his book, Noah made some words easier to spell. For example, he changed the spelling of *colour* to *color, musick* to *music,* and *plough* to *plow.*

He taught that there was only one right way to say a word. Americans were to say *perfect,* not *parfect; fetch,* not *fotch; caught,* not *cotched; ask,* not *ax; apron,* not *apurn; chimney,* not *chimbley.*

Noah put together all the words that sounded alike, like this:

be	fly
see	sky
sea	cry
tea	lie
flea	eye
key	buy

After students could sound out words of six

syllables, they were ready to read sentences like this:

Who took my penknife?
Did it lie near your inkhorn?
Do not blot your paper.
Sit down in your place and be silent.
A wise child learns to love his book.

Noah wanted American children to learn about their country while they learned their ABCs, so he included in the book a list of American towns and states and a list of important American dates.

A happy parent who had just seen Noah's speller wrote, "All men are pleased with an elegant pronunciation, and this new Spelling-Book shows children how to acquire it with ease."

Noah, too, was happy with the speller. But he had only a tiny bit of money and he had no job. He had only a tiny bit of money because most of the earnings from the speller went to pay the printer. He had no job because he thought that an important author such as Noah Webster could not go back to teaching in a little country school.

Noah's grammar book was printed in 1784.

That same year, the first 5,000 copies of his speller were sold out, and the book was printed again. Unfortunately, Noah had traded the Connecticut rights to his speller to pay the printers to print it, so he didn't earn any money no matter how many copies were sold. Other printers in other states wanted to print the speller, too. Since Noah was always in need of money, he would sell the right to print the book every few years for a few dollars. Printers got rich on Noah's book but Noah didn't. (Noah was good with words. He was terrible with money.)

By this time, Noah was 26 years old. He still hadn't paid his father back, and he was a little discouraged. But he kept on writing. In 1785, Noah's reading book was printed for the first time and his spelling book was printed for the third time. (Of course, most of the earnings went to the printer, not to Noah.)

Noah was worried about his bills, he was worried about American schools, and he was worried about America itself. At that time, there was no president, and each of the 13 states made its own rules. Noah was afraid that if America didn't have one government for all, it would fall apart into 13 separate pieces. So he wrote about the need for one central government that could make all the states follow the same rules. "We ought not think of ourselves as people of one state," he scolded, "but as Americans."

Noah thought his books were good for America. He thought that if everyone used the same books and the same spelling rules and the same way of speaking, the country would stay together. He decided to go to every state in the country and talk about his books and his ideas.

Chapter Five

Noah packed all his clothes in a small bag. He packed writing paper, extra goose quills, ink, and lots of his books in a big trunk. He told his family and friends good-bye, and in May 1785, he left Hartford.

After several days in a stagecoach, Noah was sore from head to toe. If he wasn't being tossed on top of his fellow passengers, they were being tossed on top of him. One day, on the way from Philadelphia to Baltimore, the galloping horses suddenly stopped.

"Everybody out!" the driver yelled. Noah picked himself up from the floor and climbed out. A fallen tree lay across the road. At least, thought Noah, chopping away with an ax, this isn't as bad as the hole we fell into yesterday.

By evening, the stagecoach had bumped down the dark road into Baltimore, Maryland. Noah left his bags at the boardinghouse and went to hear a lecture by a visiting scientist. In the middle of the lecture, Noah jumped up. This is the way to talk about *my* ideas, he thought. *I* can give lectures. I'll find a place, I'll put up signs. Then I'll be able to talk to many people at once!

A few days later, Noah left Baltimore to visit General George Washington at Mount Vernon. (Noah had invited himself.) He felt a little nervous as the stagecoach started out—how could he, a farmer's son, tell his ideas to America's most famous man?

The stage stopped with a jolt. "Everybody out!" Noah heard again. This time, the stagecoach was broken from the rough roads. It couldn't be fixed. Noah borrowed one of the horses, galloped back to Baltimore, rented another horse, and galloped 50 miles to Mount Vernon. Now he was not only nervous, he was late.

General and Mrs. Washington were very kind to Noah and invited him to stay for the night. Noah and the general talked about America's need for a strong government. They talked about Noah's books and his ideas on American education. Then, before General Washington was tired out from Noah's talking, Mrs. Washington set up the table for a game of whist.

The next morning after breakfast, Noah went back to Baltimore on his rented horse. Fortunately the horse knew the way, because Noah could think of nothing but his visit with General George Washington.

Noah's next stop was Charleston, South Carolina. He gave free books to every teacher he met. He knew that once people saw how good his spelling book was, they would keep using it. One boy wrote that Noah's spelling rules "stuck like a burr" in his mind. That was just where Noah wanted them.

All summer and fall, Noah went north and south, east and west. He rode horseback, he took the stagecoach, he even went some places by boat. (So many people paid to hear him speak that he could pay for the horse, the stagecoach, and the boat.) At each stop, Noah would nail up signs and put ads in the papers. Then he would set out his books and give his lectures.

"Now is the time . . . *this* is the country," he roared, ". . . let us establish a *national* language as well as a national government." Noah liked that part of his lecture best. He said it as often as he could, as loudly as he could.

In November 1786, a year and a half after he

had started his journey, Noah went home to Hartford. He had met every governor, every college president, almost every teacher, and most of the famous men in every town in the 13 United States. His speeches had been printed in newspapers everywhere he went. There was hardly anyone in the country who hadn't heard of Noah Webster.

Unhappily for Noah, meeting rich and famous men didn't make him rich and famous. In fact, Noah's pockets were practically empty. People all over America were buying his spelling book, but the money still went to the printers.

Noah was with his family for Thanksgiving. He was embarrassed that he hadn't paid his father back yet, and his father wasn't happy about it either. After Thanksgiving dinner, Noah left to seek a living—again.

Noah walked to New Haven. No jobs there. He went on to New York City. It took four days, and part of the way he walked in the snow. No jobs there. Noah went on to Philadelphia. After all, he said to himself, he couldn't take just *any* job.

On Christmas Day 1786, Noah arrived in Philadelphia. He went straight to Benjamin Franklin's house to talk about the trouble with

American spelling. Then he rented a room and began work on some new lectures about a new way of spelling.

In January, Noah was ready to give his lectures. On the evening of his first speech, Noah dressed in his best black waistcoat, with black stockings and shoes. There were only a few people waiting. "Where is everybody?" Noah asked an old man.

"Well, Mr. Webster, most folks went to see Mr. Peale's Moving Pictures." The man sat back. "The wife sent me to hear you talk."

Noah gave his lecture. He explained why *though* should be spelled *tho,* like *go* and *so,* and why *live* and *give* should be spelled *liv* and *giv,* and why *rough* and *tough* should be spelled *ruf* and *tuf.* He explained how easy it would be to spell when each letter made only one sound.

By the time Noah had finished talking, the old man was asleep.

On his way back to the boardinghouse, Noah thought about all the things he liked to do—talk, teach, read, write, study. He sighed. Not one gave him enough money to pay his bills. And the spelling ideas he talked about in his lectures were so revolutionary that nobody would accept them. He didn't put them into his spelling book.

Then Noah met Rebecca Greenleaf. He quickly fell in love with the small, dark-eyed Rebecca, making yet another problem for himself. Rebecca's family was wealthy. They did not want her to marry a poor man, no matter how famous his spelling books were.

Not long after he met Rebecca, Noah found a job as "Master of the English Language" at a new school in Philadelphia. Rebecca said it sounded just right: "Noah Webster, Jr., Esquire, Attorney-at-Law, Master of the English Language."

Noah called on Rebecca when he wasn't teaching or writing letters to newspapers or working on his spelling book. He told her he was adding pictures and little stories that taught lessons to the spelling book. And, he added proudly, the speller was so popular that the printers couldn't print it fast enough.

In May 1787, Noah had a big surprise. George Washington himself came to see him. Washington was in Philadelphia to help decide on the best kind of government for the new United States, and he remembered that Noah Webster had some good ideas. There were many questions to answer. Who would run the government? What laws should be made? Who would make them?

Noah gave Washington the papers he had written about the need for one central government. Washington and the other men who met in Philadelphia used Noah's ideas, along with many other ideas, when they talked about the kind of government that would work best. Then they wrote the Constitution of the United States.

Not everyone was happy with this new government. Some people still wanted each state to make its own rules. So the men who wrote the Constitution asked Noah to write an article explaining why the United States should have only one government for all its states.

Noah was very proud. So was Rebecca. But Rebecca's family still wouldn't let her marry a poor man, even one who was helping to build a new country.

In October, Noah moved to New York City. He sold the rights to his spelling book for the next five years and got enough money to start a magazine. He called it *The American Magazine*. Now Noah could do what he liked best—tell Americans what *he* thought they should know. He filled his magazine with articles on education and politics. "The first job of a government is the education of its children," he wrote in one article.

"Every child in America should be acquainted with his own country," another article said. He argued and lectured on page after page.

"You have a good magazine, Mr. Webster," a man wrote, "but why do you insist on being so stiff and contentious?"

Noah wrote to Rebecca about his magazine. He told her he couldn't help the way he wrote. He enjoyed a good argument, and, besides, he knew he was right.

Noah had to stop publishing his magazine after only one year. He owed more money than ever. Noah went back to Hartford and opened his law office again. When he wasn't busy, he rode to Boston to call on Rebecca.

At last Rebecca's family gave in.

Noah and Rebecca were married in October 1789, and they settled in Hartford. Rebecca soon learned that Noah had a sweet tooth. For their first Thanksgiving, she baked 3 plum puddings, 7 apple pies, and 11 pumpkin puddings. Noah was filled to the brim with pudding and happiness.

Chapter Six

When Noah's reading book was reprinted in 1787, Noah had added stories, a history of North America, a history of the American Revolution, and a geography of the United States. This made the book 372 pages long—too long and too hard for little boys and girls. So Noah wrote little books for little readers. One book began: "A was an Apple-pie made by the cook. B was a boy..."

By the end of 1790, he had written six school-books, and his spelling book was being used in every state. Noah began to earn a little money from his books, at last, but a little money wasn't enough. By 1793, he had two children, and he owed more money than ever.

Rebecca's family had an idea. Noah could go back to New York and start a newspaper that would explain what the new president, George Washington, was doing about banks and business, and France and England.

So, in December 1793, Noah started New York's first daily newspaper, the *American Minerva*. For five years, he explained and he argued. He argued with Alexander Hamilton because Hamilton wanted America to be more like England. He argued with Thomas Jefferson because Jefferson wanted America to be more like France. He explained that President Washington wanted America to be like *America*.

By 1798, Noah was worn out from arguing. He sold the newspaper and moved his family to New Haven for some peace and quiet.

Noah's idea of peace and quiet was the sound of a scratching pen. He made his spelling book better and better. He wrote new reading lessons using the names of his first five children: Emily, Julia, Harriet, Mary, and William. Later, when they came along, he added Eliza and Louisa, too. And he wrote the world's first history of diseases.

Some doctors didn't want Noah Webster writing about diseases because he wasn't a doctor. They ridiculed his ideas and called him a busybody. Noah answered politely that the study of diseases was "the business of every good citizen" and no one should "throw cold water" on it. Then he went on writing what he wanted to write.

In 1803, Noah changed the way he sold his speller. For 20 years, he had sold the right to print the book for a few dollars, and the printers could keep all the money from the thousands of copies they printed each year. But now Noah had the best printer in each state sign a contract to pay him one cent for each book the printer sold. For the first time, Noah Webster's books began to earn some money for Noah Webster.

He had an idea about the cover of the speller, too. He decided to have all the printers use the same blue paper for the outside of the book. That way, people only had to reach for the blue-backed book to get the speller they wanted.

And Noah wasn't out of ideas yet.

Back in 1780, John Adams had said it was a shame that there was no American English dictionary. The more Noah thought about this, the more he agreed. And who knew more about American words than he did? Noah Webster, Noah decided, was the man for the job.

So, for six years (he started in 1800), Noah worked on the first American English dictionary. To pay the bills, he also wrote three books on American history and geography. Noah Webster's dictionary was printed in 1806. The book had 408 pages, it cost $1.50, and not many people bought it.

Noah decided that his dictionary was too long and cost too much, so he shortened it and sold it for $1.00. This helped. Schools began to use Webster's *Compendious Dictionary of the English Language* right along with the speller with the blue cover. Not only did the dictionary contain standard English words, but it also explained American words such as *skunk, tomahawk, snowshoe, dime,* and *dollar* for the first time.

But Noah wasn't satisfied. He wanted to write a much bigger dictionary. He wanted to explain every single word in the English language. And he figured it would take only 10 years.

When Noah started his great dictionary in 1807, he had already studied 12 languages, but that wasn't enough to trace the meaning of every single word used in English. So Noah decided he had to study 8 more languages.

Noah knew he would need some help to pay his bills while he worked on this great dictionary. He asked his family, but they couldn't help. (He still hadn't paid back his father.) He asked his friends, but they couldn't help. He asked the United States Congress, but Congress couldn't help either. So, while he worked on the dictionary,

Noah also wrote and sold more schoolbooks.

In 1812, he decided it was too expensive to live in New Haven with seven children. Since America was in a new war with England, it was safer in the country anyway. So the Websters moved to a big house in Amherst, Massachusetts, where they had a garden big enough to grow all the vegetables and fruit they could eat and enough cows to give all the milk they could drink. This helped ease Noah's money problems while he worked on the dictionary.

Meanwhile, Noah's blue-backed speller was being used all over the 18 states. Every year, Noah visited his printers to check on sales. He visited country stores to be sure they had his spelling book. He visited schools to be sure children were using the book correctly. And he listened for new words to put in his dictionary.

When Noah finally finished his study of 20 languages, he had notes on what nearly every single word in English meant, where it came from, and how it was used. Twenty books lay on the round table in front of him. The floor was covered with neat piles of paper, and the piles of paper were covered with Noah's neat writing. He was ready to start his dictionary.

There was just one problem. Noah realized it would take 10 *more* years to write the dictionary. He needed more money, and he didn't have time to travel around to all his printers every year. So, in 1818, he sold the rights to his spelling book for the next 14 years to one publishing company for $20,000. For the first time, Noah had money in his pocket. He kept writing.

In 1822, the War of 1812 was long over, and Noah moved his family back to New Haven, to a new house with green venetian blinds on its 23 windows. They unpacked Noah's notes and books, and Noah kept on writing. He was only up to *H,* so he wrote faster.

In 1824, Noah took his son, William, and all his notes and sailed for Europe. France and England had more books than America did, and Noah needed to use their great libraries to finish his dictionary. One year later, as he was sitting by the fire in his room in England, Noah wrote the last meaning of the last word in his dictionary: "Zyzzogeton, a South American leaf hopper."

He wrote Rebecca to tell her how he felt when he finally finished. "[It was] difficult to hold my pen steady, . . . [but after] walking about the room a few minutes, I recovered."

Noah and William sailed for America in June. When they arrived in New Haven, Noah was astonished to see crowds of people waiting for him.

Rebecca threw her arms around her husband. "Welcome home!" she cried as the band began to play and Noah's friends filled the air with their congratulations. Rebecca and the children proudly looked on as a parade marched by, saluting Noah Webster and the first American dictionary.

After the excitement was over, Noah had everyone in his family help him read the 2,000 pages in the dictionary to be sure there were no mistakes. Meanwhile, he looked for just the right printer for his dictionary.

At last the writing, the reading, and the printing were done. In 1828, when Noah was 70 years old, his *American Dictionary of the English Language* was published.

He gave his dictionary to America with these words: "[To the American people], for their happiness and . . . learning; for their moral and religious elevation; and for the glory of my country."

AFTERWORD

Webster's dictionary quickly became *the* dictionary for Americans. Noah wrote more schoolbooks after the dictionary was finished, and he kept making his speller better and better. Every summer, he set out in his horse and buggy to visit schools, country stores, and his printers. He kept his daughters and their husbands and William busy checking on the sales of the spelling book.

When he wasn't writing or traveling, Noah sat by the fire with Rebecca in their big house with the green venetian blinds. Every afternoon, they took their grandchildren for a walk, stopped by the post office, and went home to tea and sweets.

In fact, Noah wrote so many letters to so many newspapers that most days he went to the post office twice.

One morning in May 1843, Noah got up at sunrise, as usual, and took a walk. By the time he got home, he had caught a bad cold. A few days later, at the age of 84, Noah died.

But that was not the end of Noah Webster.

When the pioneers went West in the early 1800s, Noah's blue-backed speller went with them in their covered wagons. When the Civil War ended in 1865, the newly freed slaves bought the blue-backed speller and learned to read. By the 200th anniversary of the speller in 1983, 70 to 100 million copies had been sold. And Webster's dictionary has become *the* most popular book ever printed in English, second only to the Bible. Today, Noah Webster still teaches Americans how to spell and use and say nearly every word in the English language.

MORE ABOUT NOAH WEBSTER

1. Noah did his best, but he was never able to pay his father back. In 1789, his parents had to leave their farm when they couldn't pay the mortgage.

2. The 20 languages that Noah Webster studied before writing his dictionary were French, German, Dutch, Spanish, Italian, Russian, Swedish, Danish, Greek, Latin, Hebrew, Arabic, Chaldaic, Syriac, Samaritan, Ethiopic, Persian, Irish, Armoric, and Anglo-Saxon. Later he studied Portuguese, Welsh, Gothic, early German, and early English.

3. Noah's first home still stands in West Hartford, and Connecticut Hall is the oldest building still standing at Yale. To learn more about Noah Webster, people can visit the Noah Webster Foundation in West Hartford, Connecticut.